To my wonderful friend Pat Pfeiffer,
a true servant of God

The Standard Publishing Company, Cincinnati, Ohio
A division of Standex International Corporation
Text © 1993 by Christine Harder Tangvald
Illustrations © 1993 The Standard Publishing Company
All rights reserved.
Printed in the United States of America
00 99 98 97 96 95 94   5 4 3 2

Library of Congress Catalog Card Number 92-32823
ISBN 0-7847-0035-4
Cataloging-in-Publication data available

Scripture verse adapted from *The Bible in Today's English Version*,
© 1966, 1971, 1976 by the American Bible Society. Used by permission.

THE
BEST Thing
About
Easter

Christine Harder Tangvald

What is Easter REALLY all about?
Look inside and let's find out!

illustrated by Kathy Couri

LITTLE DEER
B·O·O·K·S
PSALM 42:1

Standard Publishing
Cincinnati, Ohio

**Do you like Easter?
I DO! I think Easter is FUN!**

**I like to dye Easter eggs
all different colors—**

Pink **ones,** and Green **ones,**

and Blue **ones,** **and**

Orange **ones, and**

yellow ones.

**Which one is YOUR
favorite?**

THEN . . .

After we dye the eggs,

. . . we HIDE them!

**I love to hunt for
Easter eggs, don't you?**

Here's one, right here!

How many can you find?

Yes, I think
Easter eggs are Fun!

But Easter eggs aren't the
BEST thing about Easter!

Sometimes we have CANDY Easter eggs with soft, squishy marshmallow on the inside.

Yum,

Yum!

Yum,

Sometimes we have gooey, chewy jelly beans that taste like lemon or cherry or peppermint! Yum, yum, yum!

And sometimes we have
dark chocolate Easter bunnies
that melt in your mouth!

Yum, Yum, Yum!

I like Easter candy . . . A LOT!

But candy isn't the BEST
thing about Easter.

Did you ever pet a soft, furry bunny at Eastertime?

I did—at my uncle's farm.

Pet, pet, pet. Pat, Pat, Pat.

I like soft, furry bunnies.

Once my cousin got a fuzzy yellow duck that said,

Quack! Quack! Quack!

My other cousin got a cute
baby chick that said,

Peep,
peep, Peep!

I like furry bunnies and
    fuzzy ducks
        and cute baby chicks, don't you?

Quack!
Quack!

But bunnies and ducks and chicks
aren't the BEST thing about Easter.

Easter is in the springtime,
and guess what happens THEN!

I Run,

Run

Run

on the green, green grass,
UP the hill and DOWN the hill
in the bright, warm sunshine.

WHEE !!

Just WATCH me!

Everything is
Bursting

with new life in the springtime.

But springtime isn't the BEST thing about Easter, either.

**I like to get ALL DRESSED UP
on Easter Sunday, don't you?**

First I

scrub,
scrub,
scrub

**in the tub
and get
all clean.**

Then I Brush,
Brush, Brush

my hair.

**And then I put on my
VERY BEST CLOTHES!**

Then, at church on Easter Sunday,

we Talk
and Laugh
together,

and

we sit and sing together,

and

we listen and Pray together.

We have a treat together too.

**Oh, YES! I like getting all dressed up
and being together on Easter Sunday.**

**But even that isn't the
BEST thing about Easter.**

The very BEST THING about Easter is . . .

. . . JESUS . . .

God's own Son!

Oh, yes! JESUS is the

BEST THING
about Easter.

You see, we have
Easter because of

Jesus

Easter is about something
wonderful
that was part
of God's
AMAZING plan.

First a very sad thing happened.

Jesus died on the cross.

But guess what!

Jesus Did Not Stay Dead!

No, He Did Not!

**On the very first Easter morning,
God made Jesus ALIVE again!
The tomb was EMPTY!**

Jesus' friends were So surprised

and So happy to see him again.

"Jesus is Alive!" they said.
"He is really alive!"

**And then, a little later,
do you know what God did?**

He took Jesus

up, up, up...

**right through
a cloud into**

HEAVEN!

**It was all part of
GOD'S amazing plan!**

But the MOST amazing part of God's plan is that Jesus died and Lives Again...

for ME!

It's TRUE! Because Jesus loves Me, **you see.**

He loves You **too!**

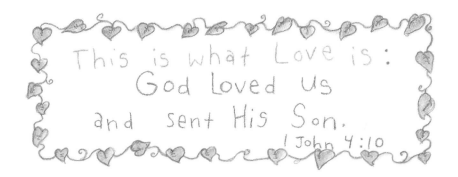

This is what Love is :
God loved us
and sent His Son.
1 John 4:10

Oh, yes!
    I like Easter eggs, and
    I like Easter candy, and
    I like soft furry bunnies and
       fuzzy baby ducks, and
    I like getting all dressed up
    and being together
    on Easter Sunday.

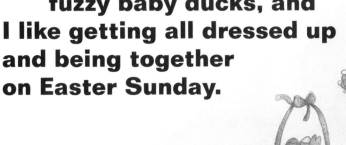

But...

. . . the BEST thing about Easter is

Jesus!

I'm GLAD
Jesus
loves
ME!

I'm really,
REALLY
glad,
aren't
you?

Happy Easter, Everyone!